VICTORIAN
COUNTRY LIFE

Janet Sacks

SHIRE PUBLICATIONS

Published in Great Britain in 2012 by Shire Publications Ltd, Midland House, West Way, Botley, Oxford OX2 0PH, United Kingdom.

44-02 23rd Street, Suite 219, Long Island City, NY 11101, USA.

E-mail: shire@shirebooks.co.uk   www.shirebooks.co.uk

A CIP catalogue record for this book is available from the British Library.

Shire Library no. 679.   ISBN-13: 978 0 74781 138 1

Janet Sacks has asserted her right under the Copyright, Designs and Patents Act, 1988, to be identified as the author of this book.

Designed by Tony Truscott Designs, Sussex, UK and typeset in Perpetua and Gill Sans.

Printed in China through Worldprint Ltd.

12 13 14 15 16   10 9 8 7 6 5 4 3 2 1

COVER IMAGE
An idealised picture of harvesting by hand. By the end of the nineteenth century, mechanisation had made harvesting less laborious.

TITLE PAGE IMAGE
This lacemaker from Buckinghamshire uses bobbins holding threads to weave the lace in a pattern marked out by pins on the pillow. The thread was wound onto the bobbin by the winder on the table.

CONTENTS PAGE IMAGE
The worker is cutting wheat with a bagging hook, which had superseded the sickle by the mid-nineteenth century. It was used to clear the edge of the field for the mechanical reaper, or for cutting wheat that had been flattened.

ACKNOWLEDGEMENTS
I would like to thank the Museum of English Rural Life, University of Reading, and in particular Caroline Benson, for supplying most of the images in this book.

We are grateful to the following organisations for permission to reproduce their copyright material:

Beamish, The Living Museum of the North, page 48; Derek Pratt Photography, pages 32 and 43; Dumfries Museum, page 50; East Lothian Council Museum Services, pages 53 and 54; Fife Council Libraries & Museums/ Kirkcaldy Museum & Art Gallery, pages 49 and 52; Herefordshire Libraries, contents page and page 40; Mary Evans Picture Library, cover; South Lanarkshire Council, page 24.

Shire Publications is supporting the Woodland Trust, the UK's leading woodland conservation charity, by funding the dedication of trees.

CONTENTS

Sutton's
Bulbs
for 1894.

THE COUNTRY ESTATE

He [the landowner] has been placed by providence in a position of authority
and dignity; and no false modesty should deter him from expressing this ...
in the character of his house.

Secular and Domestic Architecture, Present and Future, George Gilbert Scott, 1858

THE LANDED ARISTOCRACY dominated country life in the nineteenth
century. By 1870 their great estates made up a quarter of the entire
country and were concentrated in the hands of just a few families. An estate
of 10,000 acres or an income of £10,000 per annum was said to distinguish
the aristocracy from the gentry, and in the 1870s only nine hundred families
qualified as the former. Some of them were much wealthier than the
definition required; for instance, the Duke of Buccleuch held estates of over
10,000 acres in four English counties, as well as lesser estates in other
counties and in Scotland.

From the 1870s to the mid 1890s the price of wheat fell because of
American imports, and the value of arable land plummeted. Many landowners
were forced to sell. However, there were some great landowners who became
even richer by turning to industry: they exploited their estates for timber, stone
quarrying or coal mining, and they invested money in river navigations and
railways so that their goods could be more easily transported to their customers.
The Marquess of Londonderry, for example, opened several coal pits on his
Durham estate and built a seaport, Seaham Harbour, to export his coal.

As the urban population expanded, aristocrats who owned land in
London, or, to a lesser extent, in other centres, became even wealthier as the
demand for housing there became paramount. The Dukes of Westminster,
Portland and Bedford owned land in the centre of London (as the names of
some London squares reveal), making them and their descendants among
the richest families in Britain. In the late nineteenth century, speculation and
rents became a more lucrative source of income, and entrepreneurship fell
by the wayside.

Opposite:
The front of
Sutton's catalogue
for 1894 shows a
Victorian country
manor, in mock
Tudor style, with
a large garden in
which Sutton's
bulbs are making
a good show.

The local squire, usually from the landed gentry, was at the top of the social hierarchy in most villages. It was his land, rented out to tenant farmers, on which the labourers worked.

The great country houses, the seats of the landed aristocracy, became showplaces for their wealth and grew grander as the century progressed. Although fairly primitive at the start of the century, by its end the country house had embraced all that new technology had to offer – gas, electricity, heating and plumbing – and each house vied with its neighbour to be more splendid and more up to date.

There were several ways in which the well-off could do their duty by the poor: here the vicarage tea party for the village children at Chilcompton, Somerset, is in full swing.

At the start of Victoria's reign the upper classes were seen as profligate and arrogant, but they gradually became more religious and supportive of family life and domesticity, coming to be viewed as pious, philanthropic, and responsible leaders of the land.

This new piety certainly gave the women of the house something to do: reading religious books and visiting the poor were what every dutiful daughter did. Prayers were said every morning when the entire household assembled in the hall, and on Sundays they all went to church, or to the household's private chapel, if they had one. The head of the house embodied the country virtues of being a good landlord with an interest in agriculture, an excellent sportsman, and a committee member of various local societies through which he could extend his influence and patronage.

The fashionable architecture of the great house also changed along with the character of its residents. Colonnades and crenellated walls, for instance, went out of fashion: the former smacked of foreign influence, the latter of fortification, which was the antithesis of the new domesticity. Instead, the Victorians championed Tudor and Gothic architecture, essentially English styles that, as in the past, allowed the master to offer hospitality to all in his great hall. The Gothic style was associated with Christianity, with its tracery and stained glass windows reminiscent of the great cathedrals. Pious inscriptions were used in the decoration of the building. Towers became the new status symbol of the landowner, embodying dignity and power, and they were attached to many large country houses.

The champion of the Gothic style was Augustus Pugin, who had assisted Charles Barry in building the new Houses of Parliament; he designed the clock tower that houses Big Ben. He was particularly influential in the revival

Aldermaston Court was built in the mid-Victorian era in the Elizabethan style. A library indicated wealth and culture; in later years, culture gave way to sport, and the library to the billiard room.

The Library, Aldermaston Court.

of the great hall to celebrate the hospitality shown by medieval lords of the manor, who would assemble all their friends, relatives and tenants 'under the oak rafters of their capacious halls' during holy days. This kind of hospitality was offered by some nineteenth-century lords, who gave annual dances for their tenants and their servants, as well as balls to celebrate special occasions in the family. But gradually the great hall became something less formal. Writing tables began to appear in the corners – and even the occasional billiard table. By mid-century armchairs and sofas furnished the hall as a good place for house guests to make themselves comfortable, and this

Grand houses had their own ballrooms. The aristocracy held balls where young men and women of the same class could meet one another and dance under the watchful eyes of their parents.

in turn lent itself to entertainments and games. The hall had been transformed into a more informal living room.

While the hall became less formal, the drawing room became more so. This was because of two new social functions introduced by the Victorians: morning calls, and afternoon tea. Both of these took place in the drawing room. Morning calls, which actually happened in the afternoon, were courtesy calls, as Mrs Beeton explains:

> After luncheon, morning calls and visits may be made and received. These may be divided under three heads: those of ceremony, friendship, and congratulation or condolence. Visits of ceremony or courtesy … are uniformly required after dining at a friend's house, or after a ball, picnic, or any other party. These visits should be short, a stay of from fifteen to twenty minutes being quite sufficient. A lady paying a visit may remove her boa or neckerchief; but neither her shawl nor bonnet.

The institution of afternoon tea became highly popular during the Victorian era. It was said to have been introduced by Anna, Duchess of Bedford

By the end of the century, tea in summer was often taken outside in the garden. Although it was an informal occasion, people still dressed up.

(1783–1857), one of Queen Victoria's ladies-in-waiting, who suffered from 'a sinking feeling' at about four o'clock in the afternoon, no doubt because lunches had become light and supper was taken late. She would invite friends to join her for an additional afternoon meal at five o'clock at Belvoir Castle, and the ritual of afternoon tea was quickly picked up by other social hostesses.

A great estate required many servants to look after it. Many estates grew their own vegetables and fruit, and here the kitchen gardeners are at work.

Labour was still cheap, and so staff could be retained for show as well as ease of living. Although the number of household staff did not increase – approximately fifty in a grand house – the servants' wing became important as an engine of efficiency and organisation. J. J. Stevenson wrote in 1880: 'Keeping pace with our more complicated ways of living, we have not only increased the number of rooms … but have assigned to each a special use.' For instance, the servants' wing in Lynford Hall, Norfolk, built in 1856, was divided into zones belonging to the butler, the cook, the housekeeper, and the

laundry maids; areas for male and female staff were kept distinct, each having its own sleeping quarters with separate staircases.

Not only were the male and female servants to be separated as far as possible from each other, but all servants were to be kept out of sight in the main house. Robert Kerr wrote in 1865:

> The family constitute one community; the servants another... Each class is entitled to shut its door upon the other, and be alone... On both sides this privacy is highly valued.

This meant that an intricate system of back stairs had to be devised to make sure that the family did not see the housemaids going to the bedrooms, or dinner arriving at the dining room. In some grand houses servants had to flatten themselves against a wall if they saw a member of the family coming towards them, but in others the atmosphere was friendlier.

The number of chefs in the kitchen of a great house was a measure of its wealth. Kitchens were built far from the main house because of cooking smells, but they were showrooms of modern technology. They were large and lofty, with windows high up to let cooking fumes escape, and usually faced north to reduce the heat (and unfortunately the light as well). Mrs Beeton called the kitchen 'a laboratory', and it was furnished with the most up-to-date equipment. The first essential was the close range, comprising up to six ovens and several grates, set in the hearth with a tiled surround. Here most of the cooking was done, although there was often also an open hearth for spit-roasting meat. There was piped hot water, steam bain-maries for

New kitchen gadgets were plentiful in most good kitchens. Mrs Beeton was especially impressed by the mincer.

The Victorians were the first to recognise that children were entitled to a childhood. The upper classes cherished their own children, while exploiting those of the poor.

One way of keeping guests entertained was playing games. Croquet was particularly popular as it was respectable for men and women to play it together, despite the occasional glimpse of an ankle.

slow cooking, and even steam ranges for cooking vegetables. Hot cupboards on casters kept the plates and dishes warm. Among the many new kitchen gadgets, the mincer reigned supreme in Mrs Beeton's eyes: 'When cut, the meat is forced out in a perfect cascade of shreds.' But there were also apple parers, potato peelers, coffee grinders, fruit presses, sausage stuffers, and many more. There were various larders for cooked and uncooked foods, a scullery, and sometimes separate rooms for baking, and for salting and smoking fish or meat.

The family wing of the house reflected the Victorians' new domesticity as the accommodation of children became part of the design. Previously children had slept wherever it was convenient, but in the modern country house their rooms were planned to be near their parents. Nurseries might be situated on the floor above the parents' rooms, but there would be a little private stair to allow a mother to keep an eye on her children. The family wing became a self-contained unit where the family could retire; the main house became the place where they entertained.

And entertaining is what they did. Those landed aristocracy who were becoming wealthier through leasing their land and gathering rents had little to occupy their time, so house parties became a welcome antidote to boredom. In such circumstances, sport came into its own. The main house was extended to include billiard and gun rooms, while on the estate tennis courts and croquet lawns were laid out. Tennis was becoming popular in the late nineteenth century, particularly after the Wimbledon championships were introduced in 1877. Shooting, too, was coming to the fore and much encouraged by landowners, who could lease out their land for substantial sums of money; by 1900, there were 3 million acres in Scotland given over to the shooting of grouse and deer.

By the end of the nineteenth century, this pleasure-loving aristocratic family was replacing the more earnest, godly family of the middle part of the century. Country living had become less formal. The noble families who had prospered during Victoria's reign were now being joined by people who had made fortunes in business and were buying country estates. While the aristocracy's social prestige remained, their power was being challenged as they entered the twentieth century.

Sir Claude and Lady Champion de Crespigny felt that a picture of dozens of creatures killed on their estate made a fitting Christmas card.

A LABOURER'S LIFE

I think that the Tiller of the soil is the highest and oldest workman of all.
No one can do without him and the product of his hands.

I Walked by Night, L. Haggard [editor], 1935

IN RURAL SOCIETY, the farm labourer was at the bottom of the social
hierarchy; his life differed greatly from that of the big landowner, or even
the tenant farmer for whom he worked. The farmer, although lowly
compared with his landlord, lived in a substantial farmhouse, which, in
addition to living quarters, had rooms for baking, brewing, and making butter
and cheese. The farmhouse was home to sometimes as many as twenty
people: the farmer and his family, his servants, and, occasionally, a number
of unmarried farmworkers who lived in.

In contrast, the labourer lived with his family in a small, overcrowded
cottage. A report in 1865 noted that 40 per cent of cottages had only one
bedroom. Another report, in the early 1890s, suggested that two bedrooms

Whitley Park
Farm in 1860,
a comfortable
farmhouse for
a well-off farmer,
but luxurious
compared to his
workers' homes.

were more normal, but only one was a good size, while the other was small, more of a landing at the top of the staircase – which was often just a ladder. This space was insufficient for the average of six people who lived there. Beds were shared, or the family lay on straw pallets on the floor, a curtain dividing the parents from the children. In *Lark Rise to Candleford*, a trilogy of semi-autobiographical novels about rural life in the late nineteenth century, Flora Thompson describes the sleeping arrangements as:

> a tight fit, for children swarmed eight, ten, or even more in some families, and ... beds and shakedowns were often so closely packed that the inmates had to climb over one bed to get into another.

Downstairs there was only one room, with a small scullery. The barest of these was furnished with a table, a few chairs, and a potato sack covering the floor. Those who were better off might have a dresser displaying pots and pans, brass candlesticks or colourful crockery, and sometimes a picture, usually religious in nature, would hang on the wall, and a hand-made rag rug lie in front of the hearth.

A cottager sits in her parlour near the open fire used for cooking. The mugs and plates above the fireplace are Staffordshire ware.

Everyone went out into the fields and helped to gather in the harvest.

Sanitary arrangements were very primitive. The privy was situated at the bottom of the garden and shared between two or three households. In *Lark Rise*, 'it was not even an earth closet; but merely a deep pit with a seat set over it, the half-yearly emptying of which caused every door and window in the vicinity to be sealed'. Also outside was a water butt to store rainwater from the roof, but this could not meet all of the needs of the family. Water had also to be fetched from village pumps or wells, sometimes a long distance away, and the women carried back home their buckets, suspended from their shoulders by a yoke, in all weathers. As well as cooking and bathing, the water was used for laundering – not an easy task when hot water was not on tap but had to be boiled over the fire. The washing was done in a tub and then taken to a communal mangle, where a widow could earn a few pence by wringing it out.

The majority of the family's hard-earned money was spent on rent and food. The one hot meal a day was eaten when the men came back from work in the late afternoon. The adults and older children would sit round the table, the smaller ones on the floor or step – or even under the table. Mugs, wooden basins and trenchers were used for eating and drinking. In the early years of Victoria's reign, the family would go to bed when it was dark, but later, when oil lamps were in use, the older family members could sit up talking and gossiping as long as they wanted.

The staple food was bread; adults ate around 11 pounds a week, and half the weekly wages might be spent on it. At harvest time this cost was alleviated because the women and children went gleaning – picking up ears of wheat that had been missed by the horse-rake. These ears were bound together with a piece of straw and stacked by the gleaner's basket in the field. It was hard work, starting at sunrise and ending at sunset, with few rests in between, but in a good year the family could make up a fair stack over a fortnight. After threshing the wheat at home, the grain was taken to the miller for grinding; he would take some of the flour in payment and return the rest in a sack.

Bread was eaten with dripping and washed down with weak tea; but the evening meal consisted of a little bit of bacon, vegetables from the allotment, and apple dumplings in season. All these were cooked together in a big iron pot over the fire – cabbages in one net, potatoes in another, and the occasional roly-poly fruit pudding in a cloth. Timing, as always in cooking, was of the essence: each item was added to the pot according to the time it took to cook it. Very few people had their own ovens. If they wanted to bake bread, a pie or a cake, these were taken to the local baker, who put them in his oven for a small charge. And if a family was lucky enough to have a joint of meat to roast, this, too, was put into the oven with the cakes.

Fuel was costly. Coal was less expensive near coal-mining districts, but transport costs inflated the price for people in southern England. People used whatever was abundant locally, ranging from wood to gorse and heather.

This photograph by Frank Parkinson won a prize in 1902. It shows children gleaning in Lincolnshire, tedious and back-breaking work to gain a few sacks of wheat to be shared between the family and their pig.

Peat was used as fuel in Shetland. Here a Shetland crofter is weaving a kishie (basket) for carrying the peat home.

Shetland Crofter making Peat Kishie

Jersey has long been famous for its cows and their milk. Here Jersey milkmaids, wearing their traditional working clothes, are carrying their milking stools and jugs.

H. G. Allix, éditeur, Jersey

151. JERSEY — Milkmaids

These had to be collected, but were free, and this applied to some types of food as well. For instance, elderberries and cowslips were gathered for making wine. A child from Norfolk recalled that her family would gather 'all the food that was for free: watercress from running streams, rabbits, pigeons, wild raspberries, wild plums and blackberries, crab apples, hazel nuts, chestnuts, walnuts. No squirrels hoarded these more carefully than we did.' Some of these wild plants could be sold on; for instance the druggist used violets and rose hips and leaves in his potions, and was willing to pay those who collected them for him.

Milk was in short supply throughout the century. Village dairies were few and far between, and only if workers clubbed together to buy a cow could they be sure of a steady supply. Occasionally a wealthy landowner might help, such as Thomas Hare, who kept a cow for the villagers at Hook in Surrey. In any case, what milk was available was mainly used to fatten the family pig. This creature was the pride of each family and quite spoilt by them. A special mash with vegetable trimmings was cooked for it, children would gather thistles or snails as a piggy snack, and towards the end of its life the pig was fattened with expensive barley meal. If the farmer could not afford this, it was given on credit by the butcher, who claimed some of the meat when the pig was slaughtered.

When the day of the pig's slaughter had been decided, a professional pig-sticker had to be engaged. Once the deed had been done, there was the task of singeing the hairs off the hide, after which the pig was hung till the next day, when the butcher came to carve it up. A Norfolk woman remembered that 'Mother salted the hams and later sent them to be cured. She also made pork pies and chitterlings and pork cheeses, till one got rather tired of pig at last.' Pig's fry was sent round to neighbours so that they could share in the plenty. Best of all was the 'pig feast' for the extended family, when a glorious meal of oven-roasted joints, pork pies, potatoes and batter puddings was enjoyed.

Men preparing to kill a pig at Rookhope, County Durham. One of them holds an earthenware pot for collecting the blood to make black puddings.

For most families there was little left over from the farmworker's wages to buy other items that were needed in the home – and this included clothes. The extra money earned at harvest time went towards all these items. Clothes were handed down and worn until threadbare. Older brothers' and sisters' clothes were altered for the smaller children – and, if nothing else was available, a young boy might end up wearing an older sister's dress.

The country smock was worn by farm labourers at the start of the century, but by the end of it men wore collarless flannel shirts and corduroy trousers and jackets. A roomy, long-sleeved waistcoat proved useful in bagging a hare, as it almost always had a 'hare-pocket on the inside'. A hat completed the ensemble. By the end of the century, most men carried a watch.

For working in the fields, women had to have practical garments, starting with a pair of stout boots; a thick apron and shawl in winter and a

A woman woodlander sweeping outside her house in south Devon, in the 1890s.

pinafore in summer were worn to keep clothes clean, and a bonnet protected the head from the sun. Undergarments were uncomfortable but lasted for years, softening as time went by. In *Lark Rise* material was given to the girls to make into 'roomy chemises and wide-legged drawers made of unbleached calico, beautifully sewn, but without an inch of trimming; harsh but strong flannel petticoats and worsted stockings that would almost stand up with no legs in them'. On Sundays, however, when women did not work and went to church, they wore their best clothes. These came from relatives in service, who sent back parcels of clothes that their mistress might have given them. Or money for materials could have come from thrift clubs into which they paid a small amount of money each week, to be divided between the participants once a year. More often than not this money went towards buying boots for the family. Boots were expensive, and so the poorest children went barefoot in summer. The hard leather was rubbed with oil and grease to soften and waterproof it, but this did little to make the boots more

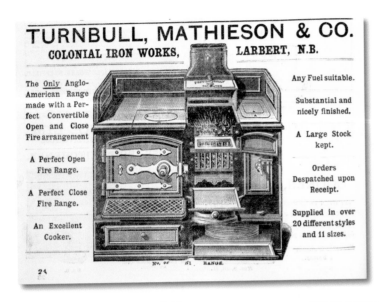

TURNBULL, MATHIESON & CO.
COLONIAL IRON WORKS,   LARBERT, N.B.

The <u>Only</u> Anglo-American Range made with a Perfect Convertible Open and Close Fire arrangement

A Perfect Open Fire Range.

A Perfect Close Fire Range.

An Excellent Cooker.

Any Fuel suitable.

Substantial and nicely finished.

A Large Stock kept.

Orders Despatched upon Receipt.

Supplied in over 20 different styles and 11 sizes.

No. or Nº1. RANGE.

24

This Larbert cast-iron cooking range was advertised in *The Ironmoger* in 1889. Ranges were produced in all sizes and became popular and affordable from the 1880s onward.

Two potato pickers pose with mattocks and part of their crop. One of them is wearing a fob watch and chain, an accessory that even a young farmworker could afford by the end of the century.

comfortable to wear, and children sometimes had to miss school because of the state of their feet.

By the end of the century, living conditions had improved for everyone. Cheap imported food enabled the farm labourer and his family to have a more plentiful and varied diet, which included tinned meat, fish, cocoa, coffee, tea, currants and sugar. Cheaper forms of lighting did away with the candle and brought in the paraffin lamp. Wood fires were replaced by coal, which gave a more even heat and led to the kitchen range; even a labourer was able to afford a small oven with two hot plates by the 1880s. With mass production, certain goods once out of reach could now be afforded, such as earthenware crockery, galvanised baths and buckets, and furniture. The farmworker was now sharing, at least in part, in the prosperity that the Victorian age had brought to Britain.

NEW PATENT "EXCELSIOR" PLOUGH.

PATENT ROYAL PRIZE DEFIANCE PLOUGH.

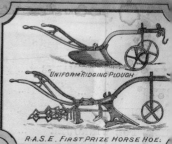

"UNIFORM RIDGING PLOUGH.

R.A.S.E. FIRST PRIZE HORSE HOE.

THOMAS CORBETT

LATE CORBETT & PEELE

THOMAS CORBETT'S GRAIN & SEED DRESSING MACHINERY HAS GAINED UPWARDS OF

T. CORBETT PATENTEE SHREWSBURY.

SIX FIRST PRIZES

HIGHEST PRIZE GOLD MEDAL AND FIRST ORDER OF MERIT AT MELBOURNE TRIALS 1881.

GRAND FIRST PRIZE GOLD MEDAL OF THE ALBANY AGL. SOCIETY GRAHAMSTOWN CAPE COLONY 1881.

ELEVEN FIRST PRIZES GOLD & SILVER

MEDALS & DIPLOMAS

MEDALS & DIPLOMAS

ONE HUNDRED & FORTY ROYAL, COLONIAL & INTERNATIONAL FIRST PRIZES SINCE 1867.

PERSEVERANCE IRON WORKS

SHREWSBURY, ENGLAND.

AWARDED OVER

SIX HUNDRED FIRST PRIZES

GOLD & SILVER MEDALS SILVER CUPS &c.,

AT THE

PRINCIPAL TRIALS

AND EXHIBITIONS OF ALL NATIONS

FOR

SUPERIOR IMPLEMENTS & MACHINERY.

CAMBRIDGE PATTERN CLOD CRUSHER.

FIRST PRIZE SEGMENT LAND ROLLER.

FIRST PRIZE LEVER CULTIVATOR.

FIRST PRIZE COLONIAL TINE HARROWS.

JUNE 1882. No. 60.

AGRICULTURAL CHANGE

The plough has the sentence of death passed on it because it is essentially imperfect.

Talpa, Chandos Wren Hoskyns, 1852

THE HEYDAY of British agriculture during Victoria's reign was in the 1850s. The landlord–tenant system worked well in comparison with European feudal estates and their peasantry. In 1855 the French author Leonce de Lavergne wrote that 'English agriculture, taken as a whole, is at this day the first in the world, and is in the way of realising further progress'.

Urban demand for food was helping the farmer become wealthy. Fresh meat, eggs and milk made farming livestock more profitable than wheat, the price of which remained static. But on mixed farms, when the price of wheat was low, it could be held back for livestock, so arable farming did not seem to be in danger.

When, in the early 1870s, cheap American grain flooded the market, it took Britain by surprise. With the development of the rail network in the United States, grain from the prairies could be taken by train to the ports, from where the new fast steamships carried it to Europe. Cheap transport was crucial to the price of wheat. The British in particular depended on American grain, purchasing around half their annual imports from the United States from 1870 to 1900. This wheat was the hard variety that made the best white flour for baking bread, and cheap white bread became available to all, including the farm labourer.

As a result, arable farming in Britain went into deep depression. Grain imports from the United States arrived at a time when British farmers were experiencing several years of wet, cold weather and smaller yields, which made their prices uncompetitive, and so many farmers went bankrupt. Those who continued to farm found a market in the expanding biscuit industry, which required the soft British wheat. Others diversified into livestock, milk production and growing vegetables and fruit.

Opposite:
The Thomas Corbett catalogue of agricultural machinery, June 1882, shows the wide range of different tools and machines available, from grain- and seed-dressing machinery to cultivators and ploughs.

Traditional farming methods were used throughout the nineteenth century. Despite mechanisation, horse power remained popular.

Sheep being sheared the old-fashioned way near Clitheroe, Lancashire. Belt-driven sheep shears appeared on the market in the 1870s, allowing smoother clipping.

Livestock was not necessarily a good choice either. Sheep farmers found that the price of their wool was being undermined by imports from Australasia, particularly as the wool produced by the merino sheep farmed there was much favoured by the textile industry. Meat producers, too, had problems when refrigeration was developed in the late 1870s, enabling meat to be imported cheaply from Australia, the United States and Argentina. However, a growing demand for meat and a distrust of frozen imports (at least in the early stage) helped boost stock-rearing – and farmers could also take advantage of cheap grain to feed their growing herds.

On the other hand, dairy farms, even the small ones, did well during the depression as the demand for milk soared. Refrigeration and the railways came to the aid of the British farmer, and the production of milk increased by 50 per cent in the last two decades of the nineteenth century. However, by then cheap imports of tinned milk and margarine were beginning to make inroads into the home manufacture of dairy products.

The most successful type of farming during the depression was growing vegetables and fruit. Imports of these were not a threat to the farmer, as there

Growing vegetables and fruit was the most stable type of farming, as fresh produce was always in demand. Here a wagon loaded with cabbages from an Essex farm is bound for London.

A leaflet advertising a mill with steel rollers for crushing oats, beans, barley and malt. The mill was produced for the Great Exhibition of 1851.

WHITMEE & CHAPMAN,
Manufacturers of
IMPROVED STEEL MILLS,
18, FENCHURCH BUILDINGS, FENCHURCH STREET,
NEAR MARK LANE,
70, ST. JOHN STREET, CLERKENWELL,
And at their MANUFACTORY, 11, Bay Street, Clerkenwell, London.

were obvious problems in bringing perishable goods from overseas, and nothing could challenge the attraction of fresh produce. As well as providing fruit and vegetables for the tables of town and city dwellers, market gardeners were also supplying the new industries of canning and preserving.

By the start of the twentieth century farming had recovered. The United States had an expanding home market to cater for and was not exporting as much, which gave a boost to British arable farmers.

During the Victorian period, farming and the manufacturing industries gradually became interdependent. At the start of Victoria's reign, farm products were sold fresh to customers, including the millers and brewers. But milling and brewing had become industrialised processes by the end of the century, so that farmers found themselves supplying factories and, at the same time, buying from factories to help increase output on their farms.

To bolster intensive cultivation, more and more fertilisers were needed in addition to manure from the farm, and the most important of these were, and still are, phosphates and nitrogen. Both of these were provided by crushed bones, and, to supply the industry, rag and bone men collected animal bones left over from meals eaten in the towns. But this was never going to be enough; soon bones were being imported, including those of soldiers who had died on the battlefields of Europe. These were treated with sulphuric acid in processing plants to produce superphosphate of lime. A new source of nitrogen came from ammonia, a waste product of the gas industry, in the form of sulphate of ammonia. With the increase in meat consumption throughout the second half of the nineteenth century, farmers had to increase the weight of their livestock; new fodder, mainly

This cattle-feeding apparatus was exhibited at the Smithfield Cattle Show, 1842, and consists of a steamer, wheelbarrow and feeding trough.

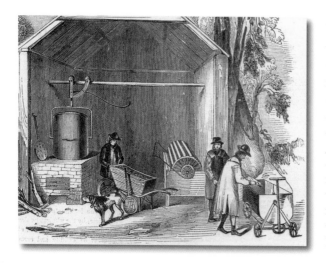

from crushed seeds made into cakes, became an increasingly popular way to supplement the diet of farm animals.

As well as buying fertilisers and animal foodstuffs, farmers were investing in new machinery to a greater or lesser extent, depending on the type of farming they did. At the beginning of Victoria's reign arable farmers began to buy simple but effective machines on a limited scale. These ranged from tined cultivators, harrows and iron ploughs for cultivating the soil, to seed drills for sowing, and horse-powered threshing machines. (It had been mechanised threshing machines that had caused the Swing Riots in 1830, where farmworkers had smashed the machines they felt were responsible for losing them work.)

By mid-century onwards the portable steam traction engine became the source of power for threshers and harvesters, especially after the Great Exhibition of 1851 in London, where American reapers made their debut and caught the eye of every canny cereal farmer. By 1871 25 per cent of cereals were cut by machine; by 1900 this had increased to 80 per cent. By then the self-binding reaper, which both cut and bound the wheat, was in use. Mowing machines were introduced during the 1850s, also by American manufacturers, and cutting the hay by machine soon became an established part of farming.

This portable steam engine is driving a threshing machine on a Berkshire farm at the end of the nineteenth century. This type of expensive machinery was usually hired from contractors.

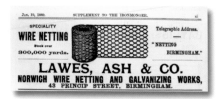

Galvanised metal came into use in the mid-nineteenth century. Among other things, it made stronger and longer-lasting wire netting.

In 1899 the agriculturalist Joseph Derby looked back at the technological developments of the century and concluded that machines 'had made the entire business of farming more pleasant and less slavish'. But the introduction of machines had not been a straightforward process; labour-saving machines were not always less expensive than using farmworkers. For dairy farms, automated equipment was costly, and it was cheaper for the farmer and his family to milk their cows by hand. In the nineteenth century mechanisation was more applicable to arable than pastoral farms because of their size and the kind of work required. While small farms could justify the expense of small machines, the larger machines had to do a lot of work to repay their cost and could be afforded only by the big estates. For instance, 12–15 acres of wheat on a farm might justify the cost of a reaping machine, but, if the farmer wanted to use an expensive steam thresher, it was hired from contractors to be used on numerous farms in the area. The visit of the travelling steam thresher established itself as an essential part of the farming year.

The development of the steam plough at first seemed like an answer to the problem of farming on clay and waterlogged soil, but steam engines proved to be too heavy to drag ploughs over the land. The first successful method of powered cultivation was developed by John Fowler of Leeds in 1863. It involved ploughing with two traction engines, each with a drum carrying cable beneath its boiler. The engines stood on either side of a field and took turns to drag back and forth a cable to which a balance plough was attached. David Greig, credited with inventing the balance plough, described its action:

A ploughing system using two steam engines pulling a four-furrow balance plough back and forth on a cable in 1868.

> All treading and compression of the soil and sub-soil associated with horse cultivation is thereby entirely avoided and the implement is driven at a much more rapid pace, throwing up the soil to a greater depth and in a loose state, enabling it to derive full benefit from the influences of the atmosphere.

After 1865, most steam ploughing and cultivation were undertaken by contractors who bought the plough and serviced several farms. The steam plough was particularly good in special circumstances, such as land clearance and potato farming (where deep tillage is required), but was not widely used.

It was not always easy to introduce new machines. The farmer had to bear in mind the attitude of his workers towards machinery; he did not want his machines sabotaged by grit in the bearings, or other shows of hostility. It was easier to employ machines in places where there was a shortage of labour, or on an expanding farm, where farmhands could be found other work to do. But during the harvest, the key earning period, it was often judicious to provide better and faster hand tools to the workers in the field; this kept wages down and people in work, which negated the necessity of investing in mechanical reapers.

The impact of new technology on farming in the Victorian period was not as great as might be supposed. Mechanisation was mainly beneficial in arable farming, but in the 1880s, in response to the depression, many farmers turned from cereals to milk production and growing fruit and vegetables, where machines were not so useful. Nonetheless, by the end of the century, 7.5 workers were needed to produce an acre of wheat using a horse plough, seed drill, reaping machine and steam thresher, as compared with eleven workers using just hand tools in the 1840s. At harvest time threshing machines came into their own, allowing tasks to be done more quickly, and freeing farmhands for other necessary work. And with the advent of machines, work on the farm became less burdensome, and the farm labourer was relieved, at least in part, of the drudgery and toil involved in his job.

The back page of the 1890 catalogue for R. Hornsby & Sons' harvesting machinery.

HARVESTING MACHINERY

THE NEW LIGHT "OPEN-BACK" STEEL FRAME BINDER

MANUFACTURED BY R. HORNSBY & SONS LIMITED. GRANTHAM, ENGLAND.

RURAL INDUSTRIES AND CRAFTS

One of the great misfortunes of England at this day is that the land has had taken away from it those employments for its women and children which were so necessary to the well-being of the agricultural labourer. The spinning, the carding, the reeling, the knitting ...

Cottage Economy, William Cobbett, 1822

'INDUSTRY' TODAY is associated with large factories near urban centres, but during the Victorian period, and certainly before, much manufacturing was sited in the countryside. The range was wide: wool was woven, spun and knitted into garments; straw was plaited into bonnets; wood was cultivated and fashioned into a range of objects; clay was dug and made into pots or bricks; stone was quarried and metals were mined; and mills ground wheat into flour. Industries sprang up wherever raw materials and a source of power – water, coal or wood – were available, and so different industries were concentrated in different areas, such as the quarrying of granite and slate in Wales, and woollen mills in Yorkshire. Some of these industries lasted well into the nineteenth century, but others were overtaken, particularly in the last quarter, by factory-made goods and cheap imports.

Farm labourers often combined their work with other occupations, such as metalworking or pottery. This was because farm work was seasonal and could be arranged around other trades: for instance, underwood was cut in winter, and brewing took place after the hop harvest. In coastal counties such as Norfolk, farmworkers turned into fishermen after the harvest was done. There were also many occupations that could be carried out at home, and women and children in particular undertook crafts such as lacemaking and straw-plaiting.

During the nineteenth century the mining of non-ferrous metals reached its zenith. The business was highly profitable as it exported throughout the world. The Pennines, where silver, lead and zinc were found, and Cornwall and Devon, the source of copper and tin, were littered with the paraphernalia of mining, the remains of which can still be seen today. However, over-exploitation

Opposite:
Two foresters felling a tree. The timber industry provided large trees for planks and beams; the underwood industry used coppicing to produce young wood for hop poles, basket-making, and such like.

led to some of the deposits running out, and the influx of less-expensive imported ore caused the demise of the mining industry, although certain mines remained open well into the twentieth century: for example, the tin mines of South Crofty and Geevor in Cornwall were closed only in the 1990s. In Cornwall and Devon attention turned to the china clay industry; by the mid-nineteenth century, china clay was increasingly being used as a raw material by the developing paper industry. At the end of the century Britain held a virtual monopoly on the supply of the mineral to the world market.

Industries based on the use of clay were widespread. Brick underwent a renaissance during the Victorian age and, wherever there were clay deposits

The winding engine at Michell's Shaft (named after the local engineer) was built at East Pool Mine, Cornwall, in 1887. This mine had a particularly rich seam of copper ore.

and fuel, bricks were manufactured, usually for local use. Small brickworks proliferated, giving employment to local people, including children. The brickworks were successful enough to be able to keep up with improvements in technology, investing in the Hoffman kiln, which saved on fuel, as well as machines to cut and to mould bricks. Clay was also used to make tiles, and, during the public-funded drainage works of 1840–70, many small rural tileworks were set up. Rural potteries, too, were allied to the clay industry, but by mid-century mass-production from the Staffordshire potteries was putting them out of business. Those that did not succumb started producing specialist wares: the Brannam Pottery in Barnstaple went from producing utilitarian objects to art wares sold by Liberty's. Farnham had been a centre of pottery since Roman times. The owner of Farnham Pottery was asked to copy a French vase around 1880, and his success led to the production of Farnham Greenware. Castleford potteries in Yorkshire went from producing high-quality products for export to cheap white earthenwares, stoneware bottles and ovenware.

Although textile mills were established by Victoria's reign, there were still rural places where hand-spinning took place, as demonstrated by this Irish spinner at her wheel.

The woodland industries were akin to farming in that they were based on the growing and harvesting of a natural product. Large trees produced timber that provided planks and beams. Underwood was produced by coppicing, whereby young wood is cut in winter close to the base of the tree, from which new shoots start in the spring; after a number of years these are ready to be cut again. When they were cropped depended on what they were used for; the young shoots of the willow or hazel, for example, were used for weaving wattle fences or in basket-making, while the shoots of trees such as oak and ash were given time to grow into long, straight poles. The coppiced wood of sweet chestnut was used for making hop poles in Kent.

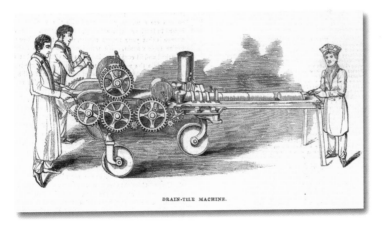

DRAIN-TILE MACHINE.

A drain-tile machine, advertised in 1842. Clay fed into one end produced an arched tile at the other, to give a 'better-formed drain'.

33

A hurdle is a portable fence made traditionally from wattle (woven split branches), often used to fold sheep. The uprights are slotted into holes in a log, and the split branches woven between them.

These workers are making besom brooms and spale baskets; the latter are closely woven from split oak (spelks). The spelk is being trimmed on a shaving horse.

However, coppicing was most important for charcoal burning, until coal superseded charcoal as a fuel for iron-smelting.

In Tadley, Hampshire, the underwood industry continued into the twentieth century. Elsie Simpson, speaking to the Tadley and District History Society, recalled that the men worked on the land, coppicing or broom-making. Her uncle's work was stripping willows. He rented rod beds, cutting them in the

winter, and leaving them in water to be stripped in the spring. Rod-stripping was an annual event, often done by women, who earned 3d for a 'bolt' of rods. But the demand died out when stripped willow could be bought from Belgium at a cheaper price.

Throughout the nineteenth century coppice products were sought after for many purposes: hazel hoops were used for barrels and hazel crate rods made up crates for pottery; birch and alder poles were important for turnery work, such as tool handles, chair and table legs, and wheel hubs. Oak bark was used in tanning hides. The left-over wood could be made into pea and bean sticks or burnt as firewood. Thomas Hardy wrote about a community based on the underwood industry in *The Woodlanders* (1887). By the end of the century, however, the industry was in decline: machinery negated the necessity of tool handles; the hop industry started using wire and did not need poles; barrels and baskets were imported at lower prices from abroad. Coppices today are managed by conservation organisations for those who want to practise rural skills.

The hop poles on this farm near Alton, Hampshire, support a system of wires that carry strings along which the hop bines are trained.

Country crafts were closely involved with farming, and the most important of them were based on the horse, which remained the farmer's main source of motive power, even when certain tasks were performed by steam-powered machines brought in for the purpose. Horses were ridden, pulled carriages and carts, and worked ploughs, and they all needed harnesses, saddles and reins. The saddler's skill lay in working with several materials: not only leather, but metal for buckles and hooks for the harness, wood for the frame of the saddle, and wool and padding to line and stuff the collar. As all these were in daily use, much of his work was in repairs.

It was the farrier who shoed horses, but gradually this job was taken over by the blacksmith, and the farrier, with his specialised knowledge of a horse's anatomy, became the veterinary surgeon of the Victorian age. The blacksmith worked in iron and so he not only made horseshoes but could perform numerous tasks important to agriculture, such as sharpening ploughshares, making nails, and manufacturing and repairing tools and the metal parts of carts, locks and guns. As the century wore on, the mechanisation of farm work gave him opportunities to expand his skills in replacing worn parts by making new ones, and in welding and repairing machinery. In some instances this was not enough to support him, and some blacksmiths diversified by selling beer or coal, or even set up a general store beside the forge.

The smith also co-operated with the wheelwright, who made the cart and wagon wheels that the smith tyred. The wheelwright often took up the millwright's function as well, re-cogging gears and dressing millstones; and he sometimes combined this with a third role, as village carpenter. In this capacity he did domestic repairs on chair and table legs, and field repairs on gates and fences. He also made coffins and acted as undertaker when a villager died. This diversification of roles was a consequence of the decline of millwrighting work as many mills fell into disuse and the growing use of factory-made items, obliging the carpenter to concentrate on doing general repairs, rather than making new items.

A blacksmith's work varied widely, from making shoes for horses, to sharpening tools, to replacing parts in the latest farm machinery.

Women and children worked from home in a number of cottage industries – which ones depended on the area in which they lived. In the Yorkshire Dales, where sheep were farmed, the women knitted stockings and jackets; in Worcestershire and Somerset, they made gloves. The two main domestic industries were straw-plaiting and lacemaking. Children learnt to plait at their mother's knee, but at the age of four were sent to a plaiting

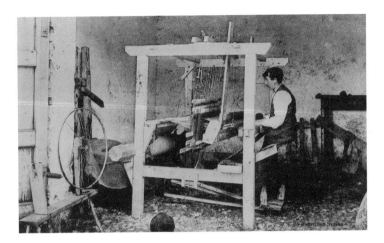

Although the power loom was in use during Victoria's reign, there was still room for the hand-weaver working on his loom at home, especially at times of high demand.

school in a local cottage, where they were made to produce as much as possible; older children had to make at least 30 yards of plait a day. Despite the small sums paid for plaiting, in mid-century an organised family could earn as much as the father who worked on a farm. By the end of the century, however, a change in fashion to smaller hats and the importing of cheaper plaits from the Far East meant that straw-plaiting was no longer viable.

Putting a metal tyre on a wooden wheel required the skills of both wheelwright and blacksmith. The wheel was held in a clamp, and the red-hot iron tyre was placed over it, then doused with water to cool it quickly and make it contract, binding it to the wheel.

This idealised view of little children at a sunny straw-plaiting school in Essex belies the conditions under which they actually worked: they were caned if they did not work fast enough, and were paid a pittance.

Lacemaking was a more skilled occupation; it required the ability to make complicated patterns by twisting and interweaving threads, and this had to be learnt. Girls of six were sent to a lace school to learn their craft, and at that age worked between four and eight hours a day; older girls of twelve to fifteen worked up to sixteen hours a day. The main centres of lacemaking were Bedfordshire and Devon; Honiton lace from Devon was the more luxurious product and was chosen by Queen Victoria for her wedding veil in 1840. Child workers in the lace industry were affected by the Factory and Workshop Act of 1867 and the Education Act of 1870, which made schooling compulsory. But the main causes of the demise of the lace industry were the relaxing of controls on imports of French, Belgian and Italian lace, and competition from machine-made products. The census in 1861 shows 26,670 people employed in making lace; by 1891 there were only 3,376.

By 1900 the lives of small rural communities had changed. Women and children no longer worked long hours in cottage industries: children attended school, and women found other jobs in towns. The nature of the smith's and wheelwright's work had altered over the century in parallel with the changes in tools and mechanisation that had also affected farms. Rural mining had been destroyed by cheap imports, and mass-production had forced the smaller potteries to diversify. The self-sufficiency that had characterised the rural community at the start of Victoria's reign had gone, and country people were working with the urban centres to process and distribute the wood and food that they grew.

GOODS FOR SALE

On the west side of this building was a broad open space full of canopied booths, tables and covered carts arranged in little streets. It was like a small city of shops.

A description of Doncaster market in *Among English Hedgerows*,
C. Johnson, 1899

AT THE START OF THE NINETEENTH CENTURY the countryside was more or less self-sufficient. The people who lived there grew their own food and made the clothes and furniture they needed, and these lasted them their lifetime. They lived out their lives without needing to visit a town or city. But this way of life was about to change. The growth of population in the towns created a demand for food and other goods, and the development of transport, especially railways, enabled the movement of goods nationwide. With an expanding economy came rising incomes, and, with a ready market to supply, the countryside was dragged into interdependency with the urban world. This worked both ways, since the means by which goods reached the countryside was also changing. Village shops were not common at that time, and local craftsmen were on hand to make boots, furniture and tools. However, for a wider range of goods, country people had traditionally been supplied by a range of itinerant traders, and this continued during much of the nineteenth century.

The king of itinerant traders was the cheapjack, who, despite his name, was better off than most of the other hawkers, reflected by the fact that he owned a wagon from which he sold his wares, which usually included crockery, cutlery, cooking pots, guns, tools and watches. He travelled during the summer months and may well have had a market stall in a town during the winter. The cheapjack who visited Lark Rise caused such excitement that they remembered his visit as 'the time that the cheap-jack came'; he was not to come again, since the people of Lark Rise had very little spare cash to spend. Nonetheless he put on a good show, keeping up 'a continual stream of jokes and anecdotes which sent his audience into fits of laughter'. And he

James Moore of Wadebridge, Cornwall, was one of the few pedlars left by the end of the century, his trade in small items overtaken by village shops.

did eventually make a sale – a rose-decorated, twenty-piece teaset, the like of which was apparently residing at Buckingham Palace – to a soldier for his bride-to-be, a deed which saved the village from losing face.

A regular visitor to Lark Rise was the tinker, who mended the leaking pots and kettles and also sharpened knives and razors. In his barrow he carried a brazier and a grindstone. He would set himself down by the side of the road to carry out his work, and all the children came to watch, particularly when he sharpened knives on the whizzing emery wheel.

For rural villages, where people had little to spend, the Scotch draper provided a solution. He sold cheap fabrics, travelling 'slowly and laboriously from town to town ... conveying huge and weighty packs on their backs', but what made buying from them attractive was their willingness to accept credit. Women could purchase material to make up into pinafores or shirts, and pay for it in weekly or monthly instalments when the draper made his rounds.

But the most common itinerant in the countryside was the pedlar. Many pedlars had taken up the trade when other work was scarce. With his backpack filled with small quantities of cheap items, he was able to sell goods that the rural poor could afford. Towards the end of the nineteenth century a Polish immigrant, Michael Marks, who was to become the founder of one of Britain's most famous stores, started his career as a pedlar. He wandered the rural byways around Leeds with a backpack containing sewing items such as wool, pins and needles, and other goods such as socks and tablecloths. He bought his goods from a wholesaler in Leeds, Isaac Dewhirst, who also lent him the money to do so. While paying back his debt in instalments, Marks could continue to stock up, until he finally managed to save enough money to rent a stall in the market. His success was a measure of his salesmanship since by that time the number of pedlars in the countryside had substantially dropped. In *Lark Rise* 'the packman, or pedlar, once a familiar figure in that part of the country, was seldom seen in the eighties'.

By late-Victorian times shops met people's needs either in the village or in towns, which now could be reached easily with improved transport. There was still room for the specialist: Jerry visited Lark Rise every Monday,

Knife-grinders and cutlers were also called upon to do a few repair jobs, such as mending an umbrella, while on their rounds.

with his cart loaded with bloaters and oranges, and Mr Wilkins, the baker, came three times a week. Some shopowners would regularly take their wares into the countryside to sell. Brough's, a Newcastle grocer, used carriers to deliver groceries to the mining villages, taking orders at the same time, and paid them a percentage of the money they collected. By this time, too, the fairs and markets that were once the mainstay of trading throughout the countryside had also undergone changes.

Farmers and merchants used to congregate at spring and autumn fairs to exchange their products, but, as demand grew with the size of population, and distribution became easier with improved transport, the great fairs lost their role as the only places to do business. Some specialist fairs, such as those listed in William Owens's *Book of Fairs*, the last edition of which was published in 1859, continued to supply a need, for instance the millinery fair at Andover or the linen fair at Carlisle. The hiring fairs, where farm labourers looked for work, lasted until the turn of the century; those held in Dorset were described by Thomas Hardy (1840–1928) in his novels *The Mayor of Casterbridge* and *Far from the Madding Crowd*. Hardy wrote that in the 1880s there were so many men looking for work that the farmer could drive a hard bargain, but the position had changed by 1902, when the farmers were 'walking about importuning the labourers to come and be hired, instead of, as formerly, the labourers anxiously entreating the stolid farmers to take them on at any pittance'.

However, in the second half of the nineteenth century fairs became places of entertainment; what had once been a diversion became the fair's *raison d'être*.

Village shops had hugely increased in number by late Victorian times, such as H. Quick's small grocery shop in Chipstable, Somerset, in the 1880s.

Sheep and cattle were driven to market along roads until the advent of the railways, when livestock could be transported by train.

On the way to market.

A typical market square, at Petersfield, Hampshire, with livestock, a range of general stalls, and some entertainment as well.

As well as waxworks and menageries, the public flocked to see peep shows, illusion booths and exhibitions of freaks, while the young men were challenged to boxing matches; and this is how fairs entered the twentieth century.

Markets were more successful in their traditional role of allowing produce to be exchanged between town and country. Market day was described by William Howitt in *The Rural Life of England*, 1838:

The Square, Petersfield

Kirkgate market in Leeds, still one of the largest in Europe, was designed by John and Joseph Leeming at the end of the nineteenth century. It replaced the previous market, which burned down in 1893.

The footpaths are filled with a handy and homely succession of pedestrians, men and women, with their baskets on their arms containing their butter, eggs, apples, mushrooms, walnuts, nuts, elderberries, blackberries, bundles of herbs, young pigeons, fowls or whatever happens to be in season.

All these people were making their way to the market town, which remained important to country folk throughout Victoria's reign and beyond.

Different types of market might be held in one town. The general market was much as it is today, offering a range of products from foodstuffs such as cheese, through pottery wares and cheap clothes, to a range of small, inexpensive items, but it was disorganised, noisy, smelly and dirty. However, open stalls where everything could be laid out and seen, and the fact that fresh produce could be sold directly to the customer, worked in its favour. The rain, cold and dark winter nights brought about the covered market; one of the first was at Liverpool in 1822, supplied with gas lighting and water. In Leeds the market was moved to covered premises in 1857. It was here in the late 1880s that Michael Marks set up his stall, with the slogan 'Don't ask the price, it's a penny!' He was so successful that by 1894 he had established several penny stalls and went into partnership with Tom Spencer.

The selling of wheat and barley took place usually once a week in the market place or at an inn. Farmers would either bring samples of their grain to market and deliver in bulk once a deal had been struck, or bring a wagon-load of grain, which could be bought there and then. West Sussex was an important grain-growing area, and in the 1830s Chichester was one of the first cities in Britain to build a corn exchange, a covered market where trading in grain could take place away from the vagaries of the weather.

Covered markets, like this one at Barnstaple, were a boon to business as people could do their shopping and negotiate deals more readily when out of the cold and rain.

As in many other towns, this was a large imposing building, designed to attract trade from rival centres. Most corn exchanges had been built by the 1870s, when the depression set in. The amount of business then declined drastically and there was no longer need for these grand buildings.

This was not true of the livestock trade, which had always been carried on in the market square or streets of a town. Hawes, in the Yorkshire Dales, became chaotic on the days of the sheep and cattle markets held in its main street. When bulls were brought to Hawes to be sold in the autumn, they were chained to rings in the wall beside the street. The railway eventually put an end to this livestock market, but not to all of them. For instance, Ovingham Goose Fair continued despite the rail link between Carlisle and Scotland, when flocks of geese were driven all the way from Cumbria to the Christmas markets of Newcastle, stopping at Ovingham to rest and fatten up. But the railways did change the nature of market facilities; livestock no longer had to be driven but could be transported by rail to wherever the farmer wanted, and purpose-built markets were established next to stations. New cattle markets were often set up by private auctioneers, as during the later Victorian era auctioneering became the main means of selling livestock.

While the expanding number of shops in market towns catered for the sophisticated tastes of the growing middle class, shops in the country made no attempt to introduce new products. They were family businesses, priding themselves on the quality of what they sold, and they knew their customers, to whom they often extended credit. Low incomes worked against expansion, as did the presence of the village shoemaker, blacksmith and carpenter. Perhaps a baker might set up shop in the village as home baking became less common, but in the second half of the nineteenth century there

When grocers in nearby towns started to deliver food to villages by cart, and take orders for their next visit, the trade of the village shop was undermined.

was real change. A sub-post office and general store appeared in even the smallest village; and the local craftsmen often took up shopkeeping, so that the saddler, for example, might sell fruit and eggs. This signalled the decline of old trades and the embracing of new roles. Rising wages enabled farm labourers to buy at least some of the new, cheaper foodstuffs and manufactured goods. By the end of the century the village shop was almost unrecognisable; it was selling branded goods such as Tate's sugar, Peak Frean biscuits, Fry's cocoa and Bovril, and advertising them on enamelled signs provided by the manufacturer. It had entered the modern world.

Co-operative societies ran shops, often in villages associated with an industry, such as Oakhill, Somerset, where there was a large brewery.

COVENTRY FAIR,

COMPOSED BY

H. NEWMAN.

LONDON: PUBLISHED BY B. WILLIAMS 19 PATERNOSTER ROW.

Pr. 4/

J. Griffiths Imp.

ENT. STA. HALL.

RURAL RECREATION

The traditions of popular leisure were objectionable on a number of grounds: they were thought to be profane and licentious – they were occasions of worldly indulgence which tempted men from a godly life.

Popular Recreations in English Society 1700–1850, R. W. Malcolmson, 1973

BEFORE THE NINETEENTH CENTURY the rural calendar had dictated the celebration of holidays in the countryside. The cycle of ploughing, sowing and reaping gave good reasons to celebrate, and related to these were the festivals of pagan origin: midwinter ceremonies associated with regeneration, and springtime ones with fertility. These were eventually taken over and modified by the Church. During the nineteenth century many of these festivals and holidays were abandoned because the industrial economy required a labourer to work, and any other activity was a waste of his time. In addition, evangelical Christians, who became prevalent in mid-century, emphasised the holiness of the Sabbath – the only day off that the farmworker had – and reviled some rural festivities. Recreation was not seen to have much value and, if it took place at all, it had to be respectable. This did not necessarily fit well with the boisterous pastimes that the labourer customarily enjoyed.

For men, the public house was the place to go in the evening, a kind of labourers' equivalent of the gentlemen's club, providing a place to chat with his friends, and to enjoy the beer, which was cheap. For those not inclined to gossip, pubs also provided games such as quoits, cribbage, skittles or dominoes, and often pubs from different villages would compete with each other. Sometimes a beer house was set up by a local tradesman, such as the blacksmith, so that the labourer had a place to go that was not frequented by his employer, the farmer. Later on in the century it was in the pub that the farmworker learned

the news of the day; the local papers are always to be found at the public house, and if he cannot read himself he hears the news from those who can... As a rule the beerhouse is the only place of amusement to which he can resort: it is his theatre, his music-hall, picture gallery, and Crystal Palace.

Opposite:
During Victorian times fairs became very popular places of entertainment.

The pub was a place where singers would perform spontaneously, perpetuating the folk songs that its customers knew and enjoyed and liked to join in.

Singing was what young servant lads did to amuse themselves, because often they were not allowed to leave the farm, even when their work was done. Fred Kitchen writes of work on a Yorkshire farm, when the lads would sing ballads about homesick soldiers or star-crossed lovers.

> I enjoyed those musical evenings singing old English songs... When we tired of singing, we told tales; at least, the men did – folk-lore tales – while I sat with my ears open and probably my mouth, taking it all in.

Several festivals and ceremonies that had been celebrated at the beginning of the century had faded away or been modified by the end of it. One of these was Plough Monday, when ploughboys drove their decorated ploughs through the streets, stopping at each house on the way; if they were not given a penny or two, they would plough up the land in front of the house. On Plough Monday (the first Monday after Twelfth Night) in Huntingdonshire there was also the ceremony of the 'straw bear': a man was entirely covered in straw and led from pub to pub; if invited in, the 'bear' would entertain the men by dancing on all fours. May Day, a traditional day of festivities throughout the

Working men often drank at a beer house rather than at the more expensive public house, where they might run into the local squire.

centuries, was originally a fertility rite, but by the late Victorian period it had become simply a celebration for children. There was a May Day procession of children to the church, led by a May Queen, or children would dance round the maypole, traditionally made from a young tree cut down and put in the ground to mark the arrival of summer.

The biggest change lay in the celebration of the harvest. The commonest custom was 'crying the mare': when all the corn had been reaped, the very last sheaf would be divided into three and plaited, and the reapers would then take it in turns to throw their reaping hooks at it from a set distance. It was seen as an honour in Wales to be the one to bring down the *caseg fedi*, or 'harvest mare'. However, the winner was also expected to carry it into the house without getting it wet, past a team of women who tried to throw water on it. If the reaper hid the 'mare' under his clothes, they would attempt to take his clothes off. If he successfully entered the house, he would receive his reward in beer or money. The 'mare' may have represented the fertility of the harvest; seed from it was sometimes mixed with the seed at planting time 'in order to teach it to grow'.

The harvest supper was a long-standing custom whereby the farmer rewarded his men for gathering in the harvest. By mid-century puritanical parsons tried to discourage these suppers since they were always

May Day became a celebration for the children, where they danced round the maypole, holding on to streamers.

accompanied by immoderate drinking and many lewd songs and rude jokes. Yet accounts of harvest suppers continued to the end of the century, when the farmer would provide a feast consisting of roast beef and mutton followed by plum pies, all washed down with copious quantities of beer or cider. There were numerous local variations, such as a visit from the guisers – heavily disguised men in costumes who would turn up and gatecrash harvest suppers in the north of England. However, harvesting became easier with mechanisation; therefore there was less to celebrate, and the harvest customs died out.

The Church replaced the traditional celebrations of harvest with the religious Harvest Festival, first introduced in the parish of Morwenstow, Cornwall, in 1843 by the Reverend Robert Stephen Hawker. He invited his parishioners to a harvest service to give thanks to God for providing such plenty. The Church of England and the nonconformist chapels began to provide an alternative recreational culture as the century progressed. As the historian James Obelkevich pointed out, a Methodist service with a stirring preacher and vigorous hymn-singing could be quite exhilarating; these acts of worship

> provided chapel-goers not only with the means of grace but also with the means of entertainment... Methodism offered a respectable counter-attraction to the beerhouse and village feast on the one hand and a more enjoyable alternative to the parish church on the other.

The emphasis was now on respectability and self-improvement, and out of this arose a new set of recreations: penny readings held in the parish reading room, where volunteers would read from authors such as Dickens; talks and debates; sewing clubs for women; the temperance society; lantern shows – and music.

Harvest home was celebrated at the seat of Sir Charles Russel, Bart, in 1863. After church, with a sermon by Charles Kingsley, a procession led to the marquee, where dinner was served to 340 labourers, waited upon by the farmers' wives. Games and sports followed.

Church and chapel brought about a change in the musical life of the rural community. The organ and choir began to dominate the Anglican church service, and hymns took over from folk songs. Many hymns were written during the Victorian age: *Hymns Ancient and Modern* was published in 1868 and is still in use today. In the second half of the century, playing in a brass band became a popular pastime, made possible 'through the publication of cheap musical scores and the invention of valves that made wind instruments easier to play'. In Bledington, Gloucestershire, the local temperance society formed a brass band, teaching boys to read music and play instruments in the Sunday school wing of the chapel, and they, like all other bands, played at festivities, such as Methodist camp meetings, all round the local area, charging a small fee for the maintenance of the instruments. By 1872 Bledington's brass band had been joined by the Chipping Norton Temperance Club Band and the Wyck Rissington Band, all playing together at the Bledington Lammas Festival.

Children were mainly catered for by the Sunday school, which not only supplemented their education by helping them to read the Bible and hymn-book, but also gave them a break from their daily routine by taking them on outings. Day excursions to the sea by wagonette, and later by train, enabled children from the countryside to visit places that their forebears in the first years of Victoria's reign had little chance of seeing, and so opened their eyes and their minds.

Children were also included in family entertainments such as the fair and the circus. The early touring circuses were small operations, staffed by a single family, and comprising a couple of acrobats, a clown, a tightrope walker, and a few horses. Sanger's, Britain's most successful

Music became very popular in Victorian times, whether it was singing in church, playing in colliery or temperance brass bands, or young ladies entertaining their family on the piano.

This Sunday school outing from Kirkcaldy to Loch Leven took place in the summer of 1901.

circus, introduced wild animals. In the late nineteenth century the circus was big business and would announce its arrival in a town with a big parade, attracting huge crowds from the neighbouring countryside. But the rural districts also might have a circus visit, as it stopped on its way to the town; Sanger described a show at Long Sutton when the circus was on its way to Norwich:

We put down a few seats and something in the shape of a ring … and announced a grand performance. We presented a lively little programme of juggling, rope-walking, trick-riding, etc…

The most popular celebration in the village was Club Day, the annual feast of the local friendly society. This was a benefit club into which small regular contributions were paid, to be drawn upon in times of trouble. The feast was usually held at Whitsun, or sometimes on Oak Apple Day (29 May – which marked Charles II's restoration to the throne). It started with a procession round the village by the members wearing coloured sashes and bearing banners, led by a brass band. This was followed by a church service and then a feast in the club room, where the members would tuck into roast beef and vegetables. To amuse the rest of the village, there were stalls, shooting galleries, coconut shies, a Punch and Judy

As technology improved, fair rides became more exciting. Here people enjoy a swing-boat ride at Rutherglen in Scotland.

Sanger's Circus announces its arrival in Tranent, East Lothian, by parading its wagons through the High Street. Travelling shows usually coincided with local fairs and galas.

show, and perhaps a lantern show, and the day ended with dancing. It seemed to typify the old rural traditions, but the difference lay in its justification honouring the very Victorian values of self-reliance and thrift.

By the end of the century the town had become more accessible to country people owing to the ease of travelling by train, bus and bicycle. As a new and more attractive world opened up to the labourer, and pastimes based on an agrarian way of life were no longer as meaningful as they had been, rural recreations were gradually abandoned, and the country dweller embraced urban mass culture.

By 1890, when this photograph was taken, there were not many dancing bears to be seen on the streets of Scottish towns, so this must have been a rare sight to the young people watching.

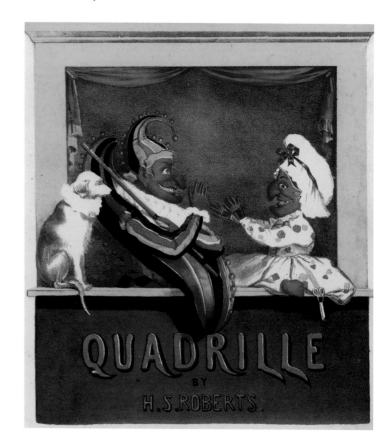

Punch and Judy shows were originally intended for adults, but they became a children's entertainment in the late Victorian era, particularly popular at the seaside.

PLACES TO VISIT

Acton Scott Historic Working Farm, Acton Scott, near Church Stretton,
Shropshire SY6 6QQ. Telephone 01694 781 307.
Website: www.actonscott.com

Beamish Museum, County Durham DH9 0RG. Telephone: 0191 370 4000
Website: www.beamish.org.uk

Black Country Living Museum, Tipton Road, Dudley DY1 4SQ.
Telephone: 0121 557 9643. Website: www.bclm.co.uk

Chiltern Open Air Museum, Newland Park, Gorelands Lane, Chalfont
St Giles, Buckinghamshire HP8 4AB. Telephone: 01494 872163.
Website: www.coam.org.uk

Kent Life, Lock Lane, Sandling, Maidstone, Kent ME14 3AU.
Telephone: 01622 763936. Website: www.kentlife.org.uk

Museum of East Anglian Life, Iliffe Way, Stowmarket, Suffolk, IP14 1DL.
Telephone: 01449 612229. Website: eastanglianlife.org.uk

Museum of English Rural Life, 6 Redlands Road, Reading, West Berkshire RG1
5EX. Telephone: 0118 378 8660. Website: www.reading.ac.uk/merl

Museum of Lincolnshire Life, Old Barracks, Burton Road, Lincoln LN1 3LY.
Telephone: 01522 528448. Website: www.lincolnshire.gov.uk/
museums/museum-of-lincolnshire-life

Museum of Rural Life, Scotland, Wester Kittochside, Philipshill Road, East
Kilbride G76 9HR. Telephone: 0300 123 6789.
Website: www.nms.ac.uk/our_museums/museum_of_rural_life.aspx

Norfolk Rural Life Museum, Beech House, Dereham, Norfolk NR20 4DR.
Telephone: 01362 860563. Website: www.inorfolk.co.uk/profile/
303286/Dereham/Norfolk-Rural-Life-Museum

The People's Story Museum, 163 Canongate Edinburgh, Midlothian EH8 8BN.
Telephone: 0131 529 4057. Website: www.edinburghmuseums.org.uk/
Venues/The-People-s-Story

Ramsey Rural Museum, Wood Lane, Ramsey, Cambridgeshire PE26 2XD.
Telephone: 01487 815715. Website: www.ramseyruralmuseum.co.uk

Rural Life Centre, Reeds Road Tilford, Farnham, Surrey GU10 2DL.
Telephone: 01252 795571. Website: www.rurallife.plus.com

Ryedale Folk Museum, Hutton-le-Hole, York, North Yorkshire YO62 6UA.
Telephone: 01751 417 367. Website: www.ryedalefolkmuseum.co.uk

Usk Rural Life Museum, The Malt Barn, New Market Street, Usk,
Monmouthshire NP15 1AU.
Telephone: 01291 673 777. Website: www.uskmuseum.org

The West Somerset Rural Life Museum, The Old School, Allerford, Minehead,
Somerset TA24 8HN. Telephone: 01643 862529.
Website: www.allerfordmuseum.org.uk

INDEX